GW01402931

Original title:

The Dance of Falling Snow

Author: Liam Sterling

ISBN HARDBACK: 978-9916-94-588-9

ISBN PAPERBACK: 978-9916-94-589-6

Whispering Currents of Snowbound Night

Snowflakes plop on my nose,
A curious tickle, I suppose.
I catch one, it melts like butter,
Then my friends all laugh and stutter.

Around we twirl, in jackets tight,
Each slip, a giggle, what a sight!
A penguin slide, I'm on the ground,
The snow just tells the best of clowns.

Echoes of Light in Winter's Cloak

A snowball's tossed, a perfect arc,
It lands on dogs who bark and bark!
They leap and bound, in snow they dive,
Best way to keep the pups alive!

The lamp post's dressed in winter's fluff,
Looks like it's had enough, quite tough!
We laugh and dance, our cheeks aglow,
As we embrace the endless flow.

Winding Roads Through Snow-laden Trees

Through trees adorned, we waddle on,
Our boots squeak like a cartoon fawn.
We stumble, slip, and laugh out loud,
    Our merry group, so silly, proud.

A snowman's hat, a lopsided grin,
    My buddy tries to fit right in!
He sinks half down, just eyes in sight,
    The jolly mess is sheer delight!

Slumbering Enchantment of the Frost

Beneath the flurries, dreams collide,
A jack-in-the-box, I try to hide.
Each time I spring, I land in white,
A frosty quest, what pure delight!

The hot cocoa brews, it's quite a show,
Marshmallows dance, like little snow.
We toast to laughter, in cups we cheer,
Let's make a toast, winter's here, my dear!

Twirling White Petals

Flakes take flight on a whim,
Making snowmen look quite dim.
They pirouette, spin and twirl,
While folks outside stumble and whirl.

Children giggle in a fight,
Each one wants to catch the light.
Snowballs fly with joyful glee,
Landing on poor old Uncle Lee.

Silence Wrapped in Crystal

A hush descends, bright and bold,
Each snowflake's story slowly told.
They whisper secrets to the ground,
While neighbors slip with grace unbound.

Feeling fancy, they glide and slide,
On icy pavements, full of pride.
But laughter echoes, as they fall,
The frozen ballet claims them all.

Ballet of the Midnight Chill

Under streetlights, bright and bold,
Fluffy dancers, white and cold.
They trip and tumble through the night,
Causing giggles with delight.

A squirrel joins in with a twirl,
Chasing flakes with a joyful whirl.
While people slip, they can't resist,
The frosty fun that swirls in mist.

Dreamlike Drifts and Whirls

Dancing dreams of chill and cheer,
Frosty fluff is now here, my dear.
Snowflakes laugh in the moon's soft glow,
Bouncing high, then falling low.

Puppies leap with joy and zest,
Rolling in white without a rest.
A magical scene, they play and bark,
As snowflakes fall, igniting spark.

Frost-kissed Echoes in Pale Light

Flakes parade with a giggle,
Twisting and twirling without a wiggle.
Snowmen chuckle from their spots,
While cats chase snowflakes like little dots.

The ground's a blanket, warm and tight,
As bundled folks venture out in delight.
A slip, a slide, oh what a sight,
It's winter's jest, a frosty bite!

Chilling Harmonies of Winter's Heart

Cold air sings, with a jolly sound,
While snowflakes flutter, swirling around.
Sleds zoom down with laughter so bright,
Parents pray for no bumps in sight!

A friendly snowball flies through the air,
Watch out, my friend, your hat's quite rare!
A tumble here, a giggle there,
Winter's fun, we just can't compare!

Frosty Fantasies on the Edge of Dawn

Morning arrives, with sparkles galore,
Pajamas still on, I shuffle for more.
Slippers like boats on a sea of white,
"Where's my coffee?" I moan, what a sight!

A family of snowflakes gather in packs,
Laughing away, no time for slack.
Watch out for the dog, he's on the attack,
With one big leap, suddenly snacks!

Celestial Notes on White Wings

Clouds release, a soft, gentle fall,
Like feathers from angels, appealing to all.
Little ones giggle, faces aglow,
As snowflakes pirouette, putting on a show.

Check out the reindeer, what's that they do?
Sliding and gliding, it's quite the view!
With mischief abloom, their party's unplanned,
In the world of crystals, they've made their stand!

Ethereal Revelry in the Cold

Flakes like confetti swirl around,
As snowflakes twirl, they hit the ground.
A chilly party in the night,
Dancing critters take to flight.

The trees wear blankets, oh so white,
While squirrels slide with pure delight.
A frosty laugh, a joyful shout,
Nature's fun in winter's clout.

Comets of the Frozen Sky

Frosty giggles ride the wind,
As snowballs fly and poorly pinned.
Little feet make quite a mess,
Wobbling like they're in a dress.

Each gust brings laughter and some slips,
Colors blend as snowman flips.
A comet's tail, or maybe more,
Just white fluff on the frozen floor.

Glistening Steps on a Silent Stage

Shiny shoes on icy ground,
Slips and skids start spinning 'round.
A snowball toss turns into flight,
While giggles echo in the night.

Like mimes in winter's frosty play,
They wiggle, waddle, then sway away.
Glistening moments, laughter shared,
In this snowy world, no one's scared.

Rhythms of the Blizzard's Breath

A blizzard shimmies, feels alive,
While frozen fairies start to jive.
With flurries prancing in the breeze,
They spin and whirl with frosty ease.

Unexpected tumbles, so much fun,
Chasing shadows, on the run.
In this chilly, snowy jest,
Winter's party is the best!

Whispers of Winter's Embrace

Tiny flakes tumble and spin,
Laughing gently, where to begin?
Snowmen wobble, hats askew,
One's got a carrot, the other two!

Sleds slide down with squeaky squeals,
A penguin gang on wheels, oh what deals!
Tumbling cheeks, rosy and bright,
Chasing snowballs in pure delight.

Hot cocoa spills from a shaky hand,
Marshmallows float like a frosty band.
Who knew winter could be so sly?
As flakes pirouette from the sky.

The frost bites gently, a ticklish tease,
Elves prance around like they're on skis.
With every twirl, they chuckle and cheer,
Winter's whimsy, oh dear, oh dear!

Fluttering Feathers from the Sky

Feathers swirling down so light,
Tickling noses, what a sight!
They land on rooftops, dance on cars,
A plump snowman reaches for the stars.

Giggling kids in puffy suits,
Chasing flurries, squeals, and hoots.
A snowball fly, a frosty brawl,
Watch out for that slippery wall!

Mittens lost in icy chase,
Frozen fingers, a frosty race.
Yet in the melee, laughter flies,
With every slip, we touch the skies.

In chaotic joy, we frolic and play,
Nature's jesters, hip hip hooray!
With each new flake that plops down low,
Winter's whimsy makes us glow.

Choreography of Frosted Dreams

A pirouette, then a slip and fall,
Snowflakes giggle at it all.
Twisting, turning, oh what grace,
But here's a tumble, right on your face!

Hot chocolate spills, a frothy cloud,
We laugh so loud, we draw a crowd.
Frosty footprints lead the way,
To frolic and play throughout the day.

Snow angels flapping, arms like wings,
Frosty joy, oh what it brings!
Moments captured, laughter so sweet,
In winter's embrace, we skip and greet.

From snowball fights to snowman builds,
Winter's humor our hearts it fills.
So join along, we dance in style,
For winter's antics, we'll laugh a while!

Celestial Flakes in Motion

Glistening bits of laughter above,
Dreams tumble, giggle, and shove.
Each flake a jest, a playful tease,
As winter's magic brings us to our knees.

Sneaky snow drifts hide the ground,
With every step, new giggles resound.
Icicles dangle like bright chandeliers,
As we chuckle, dancing through the years.

Frosty hats fly from our heads,
Landing softly like fluffy threads.
A snowflake lands right on my nose,
It tickles, muffs, then slowly goes!

With every flurry, we spin and glide,
Winter's laugh is our joyful guide.
So gather your friends, let's make some cheer,
For snowy shenanigans are finally here!

Chilling Cadence of Soft Descent

Little flakes twirl in the air,
Like lost dancers without a care.
They spin and slide, oh what a sight,
Trying to land, not quite right.

Snowmen giggle, they start to sway,
As children toss snowballs at play.
Each throw is a laugh, a joyful cheer,
Until someone slips, oh dear, oh dear!

Puffs of white jump upon my nose,
They're ticklish creatures, I suppose.
They tumble down from rooftops high,
I swear they wink as they drift by.

And as they pile up on the ground,
A fluffy carpet of joy is found.
We dance with glee in this snowy show,
Wearing big boots to stomp through the flow.

The Ethereal World Draped in Frost

Blankets of white, a cozy quilt,
Cover the world, our breath is spilt.
Snowflakes tumbling, each one unique,
Like tiny critters playing hide and seek.

With every step, a crunching sound,
A symphony of winter all around.
The trees wear hats made of crisp white,
And squirrels wonder, 'Is this alright?'

Chubby cheeks and noses red,
We build our forts with the snow we spread.
But when it's time for snowball fights,
We're dodging missiles with pure delight.

And when the sun gives a bright-eyed glance,
We slip and slide, oh, what a chance!
Laughter rings out, a joyous glee,
In this frosted land, we feel so free.

Flurries and Melodies of the Chill

Frosty whispers fill the sky,
As fluffy bits of joy float by.
They shower down in winter fun,
Like tiny giggles, one by one.

A snowplow's rumble, a playful chase,
As plump flakes fall, we quicken our pace.
We twirl around in the swirling haze,
Hoping to catch them in our gaze.

Penguins on ice with clumsy feet,
Slide and flop, oh, what a feat!
They waddle and tumble, hearts full of cheer,
While snowflakes dance without any fear.

So grab your hat, let's spin and play,
In winter's chorus, we'll find our way.
With chilly fingers, let's fling and shout,
For in this frosty fun, there's no doubt!

Soothing Tides of Snow-blanketed Slumber

Softly whisper, land of white,
Frosty dreams take gentle flight.
Beneath the snow, a world asleep,
Flakes drift down, a tender sweep.

Snowball fights burst out with glee,
As laughter echoes, wild and free.
Our noses bright like rosy charms,
We revel in winter's gentle arms.

Round the fire, tales we share,
Of snowy trips, and icy air.
While snowflakes tap upon the pane,
We chuckle at them, they're quite insane!

So let the world be glistening bright,
As we dance beneath the pale moonlight.
In winter's lap, we find our cheer,
With giggles and snowflakes, far and near.

Crystal Dominions in the Dim Light

In the shimmer, giggles take flight,
Snowflakes tumble, what a sight!
A chilly slip, a frosty race,
I land right on my rear, with grace!

Sculpting snowmen with carrot noses,
Frosty attire, look! Here it poses!
But a little bunny hops right by,
Steals my scarf, oh my, oh my!

Twinkling lights on the tree, so bold,
While I try to juggle snowballs, uncontrolled.
The dog joins in, caught in the thrill,
A powdery pup, he's got sheer skill!

Tracks of laughter, by laughter made,
In this world of white, we all invade.
A cloud of snow, we dance around,
In our winter kingdom, joy abounds!

Enchanted Drift of Winter's Essence

With gloves on hands, I trip and slip,
Otters laugh as they take a dip!
Snowflakes swirl, a frosty fight,
My hat flies off, oh what a sight!

The snowmen gossip, round and round,
With twiggy arms and carrot crowns.
"How do we keep warm in this chill?"
"We huddle close, it's all about will!"

Snowball toss, my aim's quite poor,
I hit the cat, and she makes a roar!
Chasing tails in a snowy spree,
Who knew winter could be this free?

Fairy lights twinkle like stars above,
I dance with snowflakes, oh so in love.
A winter soft shoe, my feet fly high,
As I giggle with joy, in a wintry sky!

The Softest Caress of Frozen Fleeting

When the flakes fall, laughter rings,
A slippery slope, and winter springs!
A plop, a roll, a tumbling cheer,
Oh how swift our fun can steer!

Snowball fights in cheeks of joy,
Who knew snow could be such a toy?
With each puff, we burst in glee,
Skating on dreams, wild and free!

Sleds zip past with a whoosh and swirl,
"Watch out for ice!" gives my heart a whirl.
With each soft bump, I laugh till I cry,
In this world of snow, we fly high!

Frosted windows, hot cocoa warms,
A playful scene in whimsical forms.
Each laugh, each fall, in this soft embrace,
Winter's magic brings a smile to my face!

Snow-laden Rhythms of Elysian Nights

Beneath the moon, we prance and sway,
With snowflakes dancing, leading the way.
I try to twirl, wish I could glide,
But end up face-first, snow as my guide!

Footprints muffle our giggles bright,
As frostbots march, oh what a sight!
They slip and slide, trying to fit,
Turns out, snowman's a hit or miss!

Igloos are cozy, a laugh-filled retreat,
Hot cocoa spills as we rush to our seat.
Snow-covered laughter, a treat we devour,
In this winter wonderland, we bloom like a flower!

The stars above are our disco ball,
As we frolic and tumble, we're having a ball!
With every flake, a new joke we weave,
In snow-laden dreams, it's hard to believe!

Elysian Frost on Earth

Snowflakes tumble from above,
Falling like a clumsy dove.
They tip their hats and swirl around,
Landing softly on the ground.

Sleds slide by with laughter loud,
As penguins in a hurry crowd.
Snowmen grumble, it's no fair,
They'll need a scarf to keep their hair!

Jack Frost giggles, what a sight,
Painting trees all sparkly white.
But winter's chill can't freeze a grin,
For joy comes swirling from within.

With every flake, we stifle glee,
In winter's quaint comedy.
A slip, a slide, a snowball win,
In frosty fun, let's all dive in!

Whirling Spirits of the Winter Sky

Up above, a flurry sways,
Like spirits having snowy plays.
They twirl and whirl in frosty cheer,
As giggles echo far and near.

A snowman shimmies with a grin,
While reindeer try a silly spin.
The wind begins to hum a song,
A wacky tune that can't go wrong.

Kids in mittens dash and dash,
And tumble into snow with a splash.
Each icy flake falls with a laugh,
Creating joy on winter's path.

But oh! Beware the stealthy guest,
A snowball fight? You'd never guess!
With frosty jests and playful might,
We celebrate this wacky night!

Whispers of Winter's Embrace

Hush, hear that soft, snowy sigh,
As flakes come dancing from the sky.
They twinkle bright like tiny stars,
Wobbling down like goofy cars.

A snowball's thrown, oh what a blast!
Laughter builds, it's growing fast.
Tumbling down in frosty fun,
Who knew that winter could outrun?

With every flake, a chuckle grows,
As snowflakes play their friendly shows.
Sleds zoom past, what a delight,
As winter crafts its comic night.

So gather close, let joy unfold,
In winter's tale, both warm and cold.
Laughter flies on frosty wings,
As we embrace what winter brings!

Frosted Waltz Beneath the Moonlight

The moon shines down, a silver beam,
On snowflakes dancing, like a dream.
They prance about with merry glee,
Making snow angels, 1-2-3!

A snowman's hat flies off his head,
He giggles softly, then he fled.
The night is full of jolly cheer,
As winter's joke draws ever near.

Snowflakes waltz, they softly sway,
Like children at a grand ballet.
But with each twirl, they slip and fall,
Creating laughter, one and all.

As moonlight sparkles on the scene,
Winter's laugh is heard, so keen.
So twirl and spin, let worries go,
In this frosted, funny show!

Frosty Waltz of the North

Twirl and spin, a snowman grins,
While penguins slide and the cold wind spins.
A frosty ballet on icy ground,
With snowflakes dancing all around.

The trees wear whites, a fluffy crown,
As squirrels plot to knock me down.
With snowball fights and laughter loud,
Oh what a time to feel so proud!

Chasing snowflakes, naughty and keen,
I'll catch one if you know what I mean!
But oh dear! They tickle my nose,
A giggle fits in this winter prose!

Now the snowman takes a bow,
His carrot nose as bright as a cow.
With flurries spinning in a swirl,
Join the frosty fun, give it a twirl!

Gentle Caress of Winter's Breath

The air is crisp, the cheeks are red,
As snowflakes wiggle on the sled.
Watch out! A drift is coming near,
And snowmen scare me, oh dear, oh dear!

Hot cocoa steaming, marshmallows on top,
With every sip, my worries drop.
A snowball whizz from a sneaky friend,
A winter battle that won't soon end!

The flakes with giggles, they swirl and twist,
They wink at me in the frosty mist.
I trip and tumble, a graceful fall,
Yet laughter's the winner, it conquers all!

But wait! Look there, a snow cat prance,
With frosty paws, it joins the dance.
In this chill, take it slow,
We all can laugh in this winter show!

Snowflakes' Silent Serenade

A hush falls down, the world feels bright,
As snowflakes twirl in the silver light.
They tiptoe softly, with giggles in tow,
But oh, how they tumble, to and fro!

Cardinals chirp with a joyful flair,
While snowflakes whisper, "Come join the dare!"
They tickle your nose and tease your chin,
In an icy jest, let the fun begin!

Snowy angels laugh on the ground,
With every flop, joy abounds.
As the sky drizzles down its chilly art,
A snowflake winks with a frosty heart!

So shimmy and shake in the frosty glow,
As we tumble and trip in the dazzling show.
The cold can't stop the giggles that rise,
In this white wonderland, we're all the prize!

Glimmers of a Frozen Symphony

Winter's here with a slap and a chirp,
The snowflakes giggle and dance with a burp.
They hang from branches and twirl with grace,
Taking positions, all in first place!

A snow-covered hill becomes my stage,
With pancakes of snow, I start to engage.
I tip and I topple with every glide,
Laughter erupts as I sink and slide!

Icicles hanging like frozen swords,
Challenging me with their playful chords.
But I'll take my chances, lips turned wide,
Turning winter blues into a fun ride!

The crisp winter air is filled with joy,
As kids in mittens unleash their ploy.
With a wink and a nod, we all agree,
This frozen symphony is pure glee!

A Cascade of Dreams in Winter's Grasp

Snowflakes tumble from the sky,
Falling gently, oh so sly.
They tickle noses, land on toes,
In a winter wonderland, anything goes!

Frosty hats and scarves so bright,
As snowmen dance in pure delight.
With every flake, a giggle spreads,
Chasing winter blues away like dreads!

Children laughing, cheeks so red,
Building forts and dashing ahead.
A snowball flies, a sudden thud,
Laughter echoes through the mud!

As the chill nips at our feet,
We twirl and spin with glee, oh sweet!
For in this chill, our joy does soar,
From the snowflakes, we ask for more!

Gentle Cascades of Ethereal Flakes

Tiny dancers, crisp and white,
Spinning down in sheer delight.
They land on cats, they land on dogs,
In a fluffy mess, our world just hogs!

The pitter-patter on the ground,
Makes little giggles in the sound.
With snowy hats and frosty boots,
We stomp around, our hearts in hoots!

Snowballs flying, what a sight!
One slips, falls, oh not so tight!
With merry flakes tangled in hair,
We laugh and roll without a care!

So let it snow, let winter play,
In silly games, we'll spend the day.
With each flake, joy does appear,
In this soft wonder, we have no fear!

Veils of White Under the Starry Skies

Under the stars, the snowflakes gleam,
As if nature's making a dream.
We catch them on our tongues with glee,
Issuing giggles, oh the spree!

Night frolics with a snowy cheer,
While snowmen giggle, "We're all here!"
They wear silly hats and crooked grins,
With carrot noses, where do we begin?

We sledge down hills, a fantastic dash,
Squeals of laughter like a joyful clash.
Around we whirl, in snowball fights,
Winter's mischief brings sheer delights!

So paint the night with flurry and cheer,
With each flake falling, the fun draws near.
In snow's embrace, we find our song,
In this white wonderland, we all belong!

A Lattice of Icy Impressions

Icy impressions in the park,
Laughter erupts, we hit the mark.
Snowdrifts hide our leaps and bounds,
In this winter wonder, joy surrounds!

A snowball bounces off a tree,
As kids all giggle, 'Hey, look at me!'
With rosy cheeks and silly grins,
Frosty antics, where the fun begins!

Slipping, sliding, we frolic free,
Winter whispers its secret glee.
Penguin waddles and tumble spins,
In a snowy blur, we chase our sins!

So let the flakes come down in swirls,
Where laughter dances, joy unfurls.
In this lattice of chilly glee,
We find our hearts, forever free!

Enchanted White Reverie

Gentle flakes swirl all around,
They tickle noses without a sound.
Snowmen giggle, hats askew,
Their carrot noses, oh so blue!

A fluffy friend rolls down the hill,
Skiing cows bring laughter still.
Mittens lost in the fluffy white,
Who knew cold can be such a sight?

Laughter echoes, we play tag,
In this snow, we jump and brag.
Our cheeks are rosy, smiles wide,
In this joy, we all take pride!

The world's a canvas, bright and light,
Where snowflakes dance and take to flight.
We twirl and leap, feeling so spry,
With every fall, we fly so high!

Hushed Melodies in the Cold

Whispers of snow on rooftops play,
As frosty friends frolic all day.
Squirrels in boots skitter about,
While snowballs fly, there's laughter out!

Frosty fluffs tumble from the sky,
While snowmen try to learn to fly.
A runaway sled, quick as a wink,
Left us all giggling, don't you think?

Snow angels flap in the chilly breeze,
Meanwhile, we trip on our knees.
In this wonderland, no care in sight,
We bounce and tumble, hearts feeling light!

Mittens mismatched, hats worn wrong,
Here in the blizzard, we all belong.
Cups of cocoa and marshmallows warm,
As we warm up from each snowy storm!

Celestial Choreographers

Stars above direct the scene,
Yet bunnies dance, all dressed in green.
Sprinkling snow like powdered cheer,
While cats chase flakes without a fear!

A waltz with trees, their branches sway,
As snowy frolics steal the day.
Snowflakes hop like little frogs,
While dogs leap high through fluffy logs!

Carefree giggles, a wild delight,
Trusty sleds zoom with all their might.
In a stumble, a tumble, we cheer,
A blizzard dance that brings us near!

In this frosty ballet, we find our beat,
Snowflakes twirl like a move so sweet.
As laughter fills the winter air,
This snowy frolic is beyond compare!

Glacial Waltz of the Night

Moonbeams shimmer on glistening ground,
Where giggles echo, a joyful sound.
Mice in top hats, twirl with glee,
As the snowflakes clap, look and see!

Icicles tinkle like merry bells,
While snowmen spin, casting spells.
In this winter wonderland parade,
Who knew the cold would be so well played?

Furry mittens with long string ties,
Fashion statements under the skies.
We hop and skip, take a chance,
In this sparkling world, we all dance!

Jolly old snowflakes, cascade so bright,
They twirl and giggle into the night.
With each leap, a child's delight,
In our winter's wonder, everything feels right!

Choreography of White Silence

Flakes swirl round, a waltz from above,
Noses turn red, missing warm gloves.
They pirouette down, with giggles galore,
While snowmen argue, 'Who's winning the score?'

Sleds start to zoom, a comical sight,
As kids tumble down, give snowballs a fright.
Friendly snowball fights, all in good fun,
Who knew frozen fluff could move like a bun?

Frosty flakes flutter, their moves quite bizarre,
A ballet of chaos, oh what a spar!
The ground's a stage, and laughter the tune,
Underneath the soft gaze of a sleepy moon.

With a clap and a spin, they cover the earth,
Each layer of laughter finds its own worth.
A wintery comedy, fresh and so bright,
In the spotlight of evening, all hearts take flight.

Snowflake Serenade at Dusk

As dusk painting shadows begins to unfold,
A chorus of flurries sings stories untold.
With each gentle fall, they twist and they twirl,
Like dainty ballerinas in silvered swirl.

They land on warm noses, and laugh as they go,
Shiny hats bobbing, putting on quite the show.
Frolicsome whispers float through the air,
While snowflakes conspire, with secrets to share.

Kittens watch in wonder, their eyes open wide,
As each frosty dancer takes joy in the ride.
Sliding in splendor, they giggle and freeze,
A theatrical play, created with ease.

In the heart of December, all raucous and bright,
Soft crystals envelop the world just right.
With each little shimmer, a chuckle arises,
Winter's loud laughter, in sparkling disguises.

Quiet Twirls in a Crystal Breeze

Whirling in silence, a soft snowy sigh,
Little flakes giggle as they float from the sky.
They trip on the tree limbs, then tumble to ground,
In a hush of soft chaos, their joy knows no bounds.

Frost bites our cheeks, but we laugh just the same,
As fluffy white clouds have rewritten the game.
With each little flurry, they chuckle and sway,
Creating neat patterns, come out and play!

Snowball disputes begin over who's strong,
While swirling shapes twinkle, dancing along.
The chill in the air adds to this fun,
As children dive in, their mischief begun.

So cheers to this ballet that sparkles in flight,
Where frosty your movements become pure delight.
Each snowflake's a jest, a whimsical part,
In the portrait of winter, enchanting the heart.

Glittering Flakes of Heaven's Grace

From the heavens they tumble, all twinkly and bright,
Each flake takes its chances, a chance for a flight.
We giggle together, slipping on ice,
Castles of snow built, oh, isn't that nice?

Frosty pranks whisper, 'Watch out for that drift!'
While swirls gather 'round, like a magical gift.
We dodge and we roll, in a gust that's quite bold,
With laughter exploding as snow starts to fold.

Tiny clouds shimmer, their pirouettes grand,
In this wintry world, there's mischief unplanned.
Each fabric of frostery sewn with delight,
Brings humor to dance in the still of the night.

So raise up your mittens, let's cheer for the spray,
Of glittering pieces that twirl and play.
Winter's a jester, a fool in disguise,
Sharing giggles each evening with chills and surprise.

A Tangle of Ice and Shadow

In winter's swirl, they come to play,
Little flakes in a breezy ballet.
They land on hats, on noses too,
Funny shapes, like a dog in a shoe.

They tickle kids, and make them squeal,
Falling from clouds, an icy meal.
Their giggles rise, as laughter roams,
Creating snowmen that wear odd combs.

Chasing gliders with ridiculous grace,
Sliding on grass, in a flake-filled race.
With flurries of giggles, they prance about,
In chilly chaos, there's never a doubt.

Under the stars, they twirl and glide,
Frosty friends take a slippery ride.
When the sun shines, they melt with glee,
And leave a soft puddle, just for me.

Sleepy Flourishes of Glittering Flakes

Tiny twists from the sky they tumble,
Tickling cheeks with a soft little grumble.
Each one a star, so sneaky and sly,
They land in your soup–oh my, oh my!

On rooftops they rest, with quiet delight,
Whispering secrets through the chilly night.
Chubby snowmen appear in a rush,
With carrot noses that make us all hush.

When slipping and sliding becomes a fun game,
Laughter erupts, oh who is to blame?
A frosty ballet, a slapstick delight,
With everyone dancing to a fine winter's night.

But with morning's rays, they flee with a grin,
Leaving behind snowballs, and some naughty sin.
A pinch of cold mischief in every flake,
As winter's laughter begins to awake.

The Stillness of a White Reverie

Soft whispers fall, like secrets untold,
Wrapped in white blankets, shy and bold.
Yet giggles escape from the fluffy white haze,
As kids make a snowhorse that surely won't graze.

Snowflakes wobble on mittens and hats,
As snowballs soar, like flat-footed bats.
They tumble and twirl in an unplanned skit,
The fashion of snow, they certainly outwit.

With cheeks rosy red, and scarves in a knot,
They slip from the hill, deciding the plot.
With sugarlike snow coating everything near,
Each frosty adventure brings innocent cheer.

But when the sun peaks, it steals the show,
Creating a slush that can't help but glow.
And in the drips, we find hidden clues,
Of laughter and fun from the icy amuse.

Twinkling Dreams in the Frozen Air

Glittering flakes dance all around,
A silly parade with a lovable sound.
They twist and they twirl through a sprinkle of light,
And fall on the ground, a whimsical sight.

They steal through the air, with giggles unfit,
Turning the ground into a slippery pit.
A slip and a slide, laughter on cue,
As sleds become missiles, who knew it was true?

Snow forts arise from mischievous minds,
While the world outside chuckles in kinds.
In every flake lies a giggle or two,
Making wintertime a comedy crew.

As the sun waves goodbye, and darkness rolls by,
The icy kingdom glimmers—a wink, a sigh.
With dreams of bright snowballs and frosty delight,
The fun of the cold rushes back every night.

Winter's Lullaby on a Shimmering Night

Flakes tumble down with grace,
They swirl and twirl, a frosty race.
Snowmen giggle, hats askew,
As winter's breath brings mirth anew.

Pillow fights in the cold delight,
Sledding down hills—what a sight!
Mittens fly like eager birds,
While laughter dances, bright and heard.

Icicles hang, with quirky shapes,
Frosty friends with silly capes.
Stumbling penguins slip and slide,
On this chilly, joyous ride.

Light flickers through the frozen trees,
Winter whispers on the breeze.
Grab your cocoa, here we go,
A frosty night, a cheerful show.

Silent Pirouettes in the Twilight

Tiny dancers in the night,
Spinning softly, pure delight.
Snowflakes pirouette, a sight to see,
Whispering tales of glee and spree.

Each one lands without a sound,
A chubby rabbit hops around.
Chasing shadows, making trails,
In this wonderland, fun prevails.

Not a flake shall miss the floor,
They tumble, bounce, and ask for more.
A chorus formed, icy feet tap,
In a frosty dream, we nap.

So come and join this merry scene,
With a snowball toss, we'll intervene.
Let's build a fort, and laugh out loud,
A winter's whim, a joyful crowd.

A Symphony of Frosted Delights

A tinkling sound, like silver bells,
As snowflakes fall in whirling swells.
The trees wear coats of powdered cheer,
While squirrels can't help but dance near.

Each flake a note in winter's score,
Sleighs jingle, and laughter roars.
Snowball fights, oh what a boom,
In this frosty, bustling room.

With cheeks aglow and noses red,
Twirling round, we chase ahead.
Winter's magic in every cheer,
As echoes play, it's crystal clear.

A frosty symphony, oh so sweet,
With every stomp and snowy feet.
So grab your friends, enjoy the show,
In this grand season of playful flow.

Tapestry of Ice and Light

The night is bright, a sparkly sight,
With frozen gems, a pure delight.
Every snowflake is a tiny star,
Twinkling softly, near and far.

Jack Frost tickles every tree,
With glittering coats, so fancy, whee!
Snowball warriors line the lane,
In our icy, joyful campaign.

Hippos in mittens, kangaroos glide,
All the animals come outside.
While laughter bursts like bubbles bright,
They frolic under the moonlight.

So let's parade through snowy lands,
With happy hearts and frozen hands.
This winter's eve, let's celebrate,
A tapestry of joy, oh it's great!

Lightweight Fantasies on Winter's Breath

In a fluffy white world, I see,
Snowmen bowling, just for glee.
They wobble and roll with snowball cheer,
Winter's giggles ring loud and clear.

Sleds zoom past like a jet in flight,
Kids giggle, oh what a sight!
Snowflakes dancing on noses wide,
As hot cocoa drips from joy's stride.

A snowball fight turns to a dance,
One slip leads to a winter romance.
With sliding grace, we tumble and fall,
Who knew ice could be a laughing call?

Snowflakes whisper secrets from above,
Each one hand-delivered with a shove.
In this winter land, where laughter thrives,
We twirl and play, oh how fun it drives!

Embracing the Stillness of Frozen Time

The ground is a canvas, winter's own art,
With footprints tracing a cartoonish part.
Snowflakes tickle as they land in a heap,
Why does my nose feel like it's trying to peep?

Snowball battles turn to snowy regrets,
Who knew that ice could be such big threats?
With a laugh and a stumble, we're caught in a bind,
The snow-dusted clown, am I ever so blind!

A snowman sneezes, oh what a sight,
His carrot nose shudders, a hilarious fright.
With a scarf unwrapped and a hat on awry,
He seems to shout, "Give me a pie!"

Crisp air fills lungs with a giggling cheer,
As each frosty puff brings new joy near.
We embrace the stillness, so charming and bright,
In this frozen wonder, our hearts take flight!

Snowbound Revelry

A snowman with a crooked hat,
He wobbles while he practices that.
The flakes fall down, a snowy kiss,
He slips and falls; oh, what a miss!

A snowball fight, it's pure delight,
With friendly fire, we chase the light.
Laughter echoes through the chill,
As snowflakes dance, we can't sit still!

Snowflakes land on puppy's nose,
He sneezes once, then off he goes.
In fluffy coats, we parade about,
Making snow angels, giggling out loud!

Oh dear, a snowdrift blocks the way,
We climb and slip, with kids at play.
But every tumble brings a cheer,
Winter fun, it's all so near!

Twinkling Shadows on a Winter's Day

In the frosty air, we prance and sway,
With boots that squeak in a funny way.
Our shadows stretch, a wobbly sight,
Twinkling with glee in the morning light.

The snowflakes tickle, a silly tease,
As we catch them with playful ease.
A snowdrift's throne, I take a seat,
But whoops! I slide right off my feet!

A cartwheel crash, a flurry of fun,
We race around, but who's the fastest one?
The icicles dangle like goofy hats,
While snowmen stand like chubby cats.

With scarves that flap and mittens bright,
We frolic 'til the fall of night.
Oh winter's whimsy, a giggling spree,
In sparkling clouds, we laugh with glee!

Crystal Cascades

The roof's a stage for a snowy show,
Icicles swinging, dipping low.
They sparkle bright in the winter sun,
While squirrel acrobatics just begun!

Snowflakes tumble, a slippery slide,
I take a leap, oh what a ride!
A twist, a turn, a spin and fall,
My belly whirls, I'm having a ball!

The trees wear coats of glistening white,
As we build forts, the snowball fight.
With every throw, laughter bursts,
The winter chill, it only spurs!

A snow-plow roars, the fun won't cease,
As kids rush out, their energy increase.
With frosty giggles filling the air,
These crystal cascades, beyond compare!

Threads of Icy Euphoria

In cozy hats and mittens tight,
We prance about in pure delight.
Snowflakes twirl in a frisky spree,
Calling out, "Come, play with me!"

A plump snowman, his eyes askew,
Seems to chuckle at me and you.
With snowball launchers all around,
It's snowy chaos, laughter abounds!

A puppy leaps through the snowy drifts,
Chasing shadows as his spirit lifts.
He tumbles down in fluff and fun,
Not caring how he just begun!

Sledding thrills on a hilltop high,
With squeals of joy that reach the sky.
Oh, laughter flies with each swift ride,
In threads of joy, we take our stride!

Midnight Waltz of Whispering Winds

The wind twirls in silly spins,
Tickling branches, laughing grins.
Snowflakes leap and hop around,
Like ballet stars without a sound.

Streetlamps wink, their shadows play,
While snowflakes dance in disarray.
A swirling jig, a frosty breeze,
Even the trees sway with ease.

Children giggle as they slide,
On icy paths, with joy as guide.
With hats askew and scarves untied,
In this cold, we take our pride.

So let us twirl through frozen air,
With laughter bright, without a care.
In a world where snowflakes tease,
Our midnight waltz, a winter breeze.

Frosty Feathers Falling Like Dreams

Feathers float from lofty heights,
They tumble down in playful flights.
One lands on a nose so red,
Causing giggles, joy widespread.

A snowman grins with carrot charm,
While snowflakes dance without alarm.
They bump and bounce like silly clowns,
Covering all the sleepy towns.

A puppy leaps, a frosty paw,
Chasing flakes, and oh, what a jaw!
With frosty breath, they shimmer bright,
Together, making pure delight.

So let's enjoy this chilly spree,
Like little birds, wild and free.
With laughter ringing through the air,
Let's catch the dreams, beyond compare!

Winter's Shadowed Dance in Twilight

As twilight falls, the shadows play,
With snowflakes tumbling, bright display.
A cat slips by, the jester's pounce,
Chasing flurries, round and round.

Icicles dangle, all absurd,
Like comedy scripts without a word.
Under the moon, they shimmer bright,
Twinkling softly in the night.

Whispers of laughter in the cold,
As winter softens, stories told.
They twirl and sway, a frosty show,
Inviting all to join the flow.

So grab a friend, let worries go,
Together in this chilly glow.
With every leap, a silly prance,
In winter's arms, let's take the chance!

Glistening Ribbons of Quiet Grace

Ribbons of white, they swirl and glide,
With hiccuped puffs, they twist and slide.
Over rooftops, like playful elves,
Joining in a dance by themselves.

Sprightly flakes parade in rows,
As giggles hitch a frosty pose.
A flock of birds in a snowy spree,
Making mischief, wild and free.

Sleds go zooming, laughter bursts,
With every plunge, the joy rehearsed.
In this frozen, false ballet,
We find our cheer in playful play.

So grab your mittens, join the fun,
Chasing snowflakes 'til the day is done.
In this grand spectacle of white,
Together we'll dance through the night!

The Serenade of Icy Whispers

Snowflakes tiptoe from the sky,
They pirouette, oh my, oh my!
Each flake tries to steal the show,
But lands on a nose, what a blow!

Squirrels in coats, they frolic and twirl,
Chasing each other in a dizzy whirl.
A drifted mound, a perfect tall tower,
They leap, they dive, then crash with power!

The pitter-patter is quite a feat,
As little feet run in fast retreat.
Giggles erupt as they slip around,
Snow angels making a silly sound!

Oh frosty day, please stay awhile,
As snowmen grin with a giant smile.
A world blanketed, so soft and bright,
Turns weary frowns to pure delight!

Glacial Patterns in Ghostly Glow

The moonlight winks, it's quite the sight,
While ice sculptures have their own delight.
A penguin waddles, trying to slide,
With flapping wings, he's full of pride!

Snowflakes gather, plotting and scheming,
On rooftops high, they're all just dreaming.
A blizzard's coming, they cheer and shout,
"Let's pile it high! Don't leave a doubt!"

Kids in groups launch a snowball spree,
But someone hides behind a tree.
With a cheeky grin, they spring a trap,
And a flurry of snow will cause a clap!

With hot cocoa in endless supply,
We raise our mugs, it's time to fly!
Laughter echoes through winter's glow,
As frosty fun makes spirits grow!

Magic Drift of Winter's Kiss

Oh, watch the snowflakes dance on down,
Twisting, turning without a frown.
They tease the cats who chase with glee,
While squirrels plot the next big spree!

A snowman wears a hat too large,
He drifts along, a jolly charge.
With buttons crooked, and a carrot nose,
He's dancing too, in winter's prose!

A clumsy slip, a hearty fall,
The laughter echoes through it all.
As snow shovels become slidey toys,
A wintry ruckus among the boys!

The winter air is crisp and bright,
With giggles mingling in the night.
Snowflakes swirl like a silly kiss,
Creating moments that none would miss!

Frosty Canvases in the Quiet Night

Blankets of white cover the halls,
As winter's charm gives chilly calls.
The neighborhood's alive with cheer,
As laughter rings, bringing friends near!

Puppies tumble in a snowy haze,
Fluffy faces, in a playful craze.
They leap and bound, a happy sight,
Creating joy in the frosty night!

Giant snowballs roll with glee,
Building forts as proud as can be.
But oops! Here comes a stormy blast,
And down go walls—all fun amassed!

The stars twinkle, twinkling bright,
While snowflakes dance in pure delight.
A tapestry woven through the dark,
In winter's glow, we leave our mark!

Swaying Trees in the Chill of Night

Twirl and twizzle, oh what a sight,
Branches wave like they're in flight,
Squirrels giggle, what a delight,
As winter's breath brings them to light.

With hats made of snow, they dance on high,
While chilly winds make the branches sigh,
The trees take bows, oh so spry,
While giggling snowflakes float on by.

Beneath the moon, their shadows play,
A leafy waltz on a snowy tray,
The forest's humor on full display,
As winter nights wear a sparkling fray.

In the frosty air, a playful cheer,
The trees sway gently, spreading good cheer,
Whispering secrets for all to hear,
In the chilly night, they've nothing to fear.

Luminescent Ballet of the Storm

Whirling winds with a spun-out twirl,
Lightning leaps and the raindrops swirl,
Clouds throw shade, as if to hurl,
A zany show in a stormy whirl.

Puddles splash like dancers on stage,
A wacky storm pulls the crowds in rage,
Nature laughs, turning each page,
As chaos blooms, it's all the rage.

Frogs in tuxedos hop with flair,
While light shows dazzle, up in the air,
Each clap of thunder, a funky dare,
In the tempest's midst, laughter's rare.

They leap and bound, joyfully tossed,
In this funny ballet, no one gets lost,
For when storms come, laughter's the cost,
In nature's theater, merriment glossed.

Embracing Shadows in the Snowfall

Whimsical shapes in the silver light,
Shadows jiggle, what a funny sight,
Skiers tumble, oh what a bite,
As blankets of white make the world so bright.

Snowflakes drift with a giggly grace,
Painting cheeks in a frosty embrace,
Each whoosh and tumble, a playful chase,
As winter skies wear a glimmering lace.

Through puffs of snow, the laughter flows,
With every step, the mischief grows,
Chasing snowmen as each one glows,
In a wacky game where the merriment shows.

In the frosty depths of winter's charm,
Every fall brings its own warm balm,
With giggles echoing, sweet and calm,
In this snowy realm, joy is the norm.

Crystal Revelations in the Stillness

Amidst the quiet, a sparkle appears,
Icicles dangle like whimsical spears,
Nature's laughter whispers in ears,
As frosty fingers brush away fears.

Crystals glisten, a shining brigade,
Winter's jewels in a sparkly parade,
Snowmen wobble, their hats unmade,
In this frosted world, fun is portrayed.

Each snowflake's giggle, a note in the air,
Dancing like crazy without a care,
With chilly whispers, they all declare,
Life's a grand party, nothing is rare.

In the stillness where silence reigns,
Funny little quirks burst through the pains,
Amidst the shimmer, mischief remains,
As laughter sparkles on winter's chains.

Cosmic Drift of the Flurries

Snowflakes twirl in silly spins,
They wobble like a dancing kin.
With every gust they whip and swirl,
Like giggling friends in a twirling whirl.

They tangle up like tangled hair,
In hats and mittens, they have no care.
A frosty joke, a winter's jest,
Slipping and sliding, they do their best.

The ground a canvas, white and bright,
They paint with laughter, pure delight.
As winter's cry becomes a cheer,
Nature's jesters having fun here.

So grab your sled, let's take a ride,
On icy lanes, let's slip and slide.
In frosty air, we hear the sound,
Of flurries laughing all around.

Snowbound Elegy

Once upon a snowflake's fall,
Chilled whispers danced amidst it all.
They plotted softly, made a mess,
In coats too tight, they did confess.

A snowman grinned with button eyes,
He lost a nose and felt unwise.
In frozen pose, he tried to flex,
But topped with snow, he found his Rex.

A squirrel in boots found no delight,
As he slipped and flipped in frosty flight.
His acorns buried, oh what a fate,
Chasing dreams while snowflakes skate.

Each flake a dancer on a string,
Wiggling lightly, giggling bling.
When winter bows, they'll have their say,
In fluffy silence, they'll drift away.

Grace of the Winter Veil

A blanket soft on frozen ground,
Whispers giggles in the sound.
Upward they leap, those flakes, so spry,
As if they know how to jump and fly.

In cozy nooks, hot cocoa brews,
While snowflakes plan their next big moves.
With tippy toes, they pirouette,
Creating chaos without regret.

A flurry's wink, a twinkling light,
Tempting sledders with snowy might.
They cheer on children who tumble down,
In a parade of laughter, laugh out loud!

Winter's riot, a whimsical tease,
They frolic and glide with frosty ease.
As giggles echo, their mission clear,
To spread the joy year after year.

Ethereal Veils Descending

In sheer delight, they twinkle down,
As winter slips on its frosty gown.
They flicker here and skitter there,
Like playful faeries in the air.

A snowball fight turns into fun,
With puffs and giggles, no one can run.
Flake after flake, a world of white,
Comedic chaos takes its flight.

Their frosty frolics, a merry spree,
Dancing through trees, just wait and see.
Spinning, laughing, they lose their way,
Landing on puppies who love to play.

As winter wraps its fluffy shawl,
Each icy jester beckons all.
Join the fun, don't miss the show,
With every flurry, laughter will grow.

Twinkling Moments on a Frozen Lake

Snowflakes jump and twist in glee,
A waltz upon the ice, you see.
Penguins try their fanciest prance,
While squirrels join in, keen to dance.

The frosty air is filled with cheer,
As grumpy old snowmen slouch near.
They grumble at the playful sight,
Yet secretly they love the night.

Children giggle, scattered and bold,
Building snow forts, warriors of gold.
With snowballs flying through the air,
Laughter echoes everywhere!

So grab a partner, here we go!
On slippery patches, we all flow.
In this winter's merry dome,
Let's dance until we all go home!

Whirlwinds of Frosted Glimmer

Round and round, the flakes do spin,
Tickling noses, under skin.
Lively spirits whirl about,
With every snowflake, there's a shout!

Cats in sweaters, prancing proud,
Look like jesters from a crowd.
While dogs leap to catch on high,
As flakes land softly from the sky.

Chilly cheeks and frosty toes,
Slip on ice, oh how it goes!
Trip and tumble, what a sight,
Creating giggles, pure delight.

Glimmering cold, the world's aglow,
Happiness blooms in the frosty flow.
So chase those flakes, don't hold back,
In this whimsical winter track!

A Journey Through Silver Dusk

As daylight fades, we shall embark,
On snowy paths where all is stark.
Mittens mismatched, hats askew,
Each step a blessing, fresh and new.

Sideways glances, a slip or trip,
In our journey, there's no script.
Snowmen chuckle, with noses long,
Listening in as we sing our song.

With frosty breath, we start to race,
And soon enough, we fall from grace.
But laughter bubbles through the night,
As we brush off snow, feeling light.

So grab your pals, don't linger long,
Dance through this dusk, we can't go wrong!
Every tumble brings a grin,
So keep on laughing, let's begin!

Glimmers of White in the Late Evening

Under the streetlight's golden glow,
Tiny twirls of white do flow.
Bumbling figures all around,
With playful shouts, wintery sound.

Ice skates squeak like happy mice,
As awkward stumbles twist like dice.
Hot cocoa spills, a sweet surprise,
While marshmallows float like fluffy skies.

A snowball fight breaks out at last,
With laughter ringing, time flies fast.
Even the moon can't help but smile,
Watching all the fun and style.

So gather 'round, both young and old,
In this wonderland, brave and bold.
Let's cherish glimmers, spark and shine,
Winter's delight, forever divine!

Milton Keynes UK
Ingram Content Group UK Ltd.
UKHW030749121124
451094UK00013B/835

9 789916 945896